HEARTBEATS & HUGS

THE STORY OF APOLLO, SWEETEST POODLE WHO EVER LIVED

DR. MONICA YOUNG ANDREWS

Illustrated by
LOVELIGHT INTERNATIONAL PRESS

CONTENTS

Heartbeats & Hugs — v

The Story of Apollo, Sweetest Poodle who ever lived — 1

In Memory Of — 21
About the Author — 23

HEARTBEATS & HUGS

THE STORY OF APOLLO

Sweetest Poodle Who Ever Lived

Dr. Monica Young Andrews

Copyright © 2020 – Dr. Monica Young Andrews

All rights reserved. This book is protected by the copyright laws of the United States of America. This book may not be copied or reprinted for commercial gain or profit. The use of quotations or occasional page copying for personal or group study is permitted and encouraged. Permission will be granted upon request.

Hard cover ISBN: 978-1-7355168-1-3

Library of Congress Cataloging-in-Publication Data

Names: Andrews, Dr. Monica Young

Title: Heartbeats & Hugs: The Story of Apollo, Sweetest Poodle Who Ever Lived / Library of Congress Control Number: 2020921613

Dr. Monica Young Andrews / Divine Order, Perry Hall, Maryland

www.divineordernetwork.com

Illustrator, Publishing & Editor Consultant:

Lovelight International Press

Proceeds donated to:

Divine Order Foundation, Perry Hall, Maryland

This heartfelt dedication is…
To De'Vaughn Jenkins & Vincent Jenkins as I would have not had a dog if it were not for the both of you;

*To Rachelle Roberts, Sean Andrews, Jordan Andrews, Lauren A. Andrews, Rose Thurston, Pamela Cousins, Samirah Brown, Debbie & Dominique White, Lorraine Lansey, Kathy Kline, Lauren P. Andrews, the late Ronald W. Andrews aka Grandfather, Laura Littlefield, Brenadette Andrews as I would not have **kept** a dog if it were not for all of you;*

To Dr. judi Love bowman as this writing would not have been completed without you & Lovelight International Press

THE STORY OF APOLLO, SWEETEST POODLE WHO EVER LIVED

Hi, I'm Apollo, a black miniature poodle. I was born (or whelped as my papers say) Friday, April 8, 2005.

They say I was the "runt" of the bunch. That means I was the smallest or weakest of my litter of brothers and sisters.

It was cool the way I connected with my new family. When my breeder met a family of three: father, mother and son, in a small parking lot, I was sooooo scared that when I was put on the ground, I just sat there and trembled. The great thing was that there were only two of us: a white Maltese (who was very fun and playful I even had to admit) and little ole' me.

The two guys went for the Maltese; but the lady came and scooped me up while doing something so comforting to me. She put my head up against her heart and stroked me. Wow! I hadn't EVER felt that comfortable!

DR. MONICA YOUNG ANDREWS

I learned to really love that sentimental behavior. Each day I'd get in her arms one way or another and rest my head against her chest so I could hear her heartbeat. And you know what, I soon noticed that she had her hand against my chest holding me up and could hear my heartbeat, too! Wow! That was so cool!

Early on there was trouble with my ears. I had terrible ear infections. It was a good thing that my mommy found a colloidal silver product called Peace & Kindness by Chris Christensen. That blue spray bottle saved all of us years of time and money as we never had to worry about my ears ever being infected again. She even uses it on herself and other loved ones.

HEARTBEATS & HUGS

My daddy took me to Banfield Pet Hospital for their wellness care program. He enrolled me and bought me everything I needed from the store. The thing I like most about going to Banfield is that they are mostly located in PetSmart stores. PetSmart has everything for all kinds of pets!
It's funny when I'd go in the pet store on my leash with my mother, father, or big brother, my feet always seemed to slide across the floor. I felt as if I were ice skating.

I was always super delighted to slide up and down the aisles and exchange glances and sniffs with my doggie "friends" and their families. I always got a special treat after leaving there and looked forward to our visits even if

DR. MONICA YOUNG ANDREWS

I was left to get a haircut and bath. I loved the way the peppermint bath soap smelled.

My big brother DeVaughn showed me lots of tricks. I could sit, lay down and roll over. I always looked forward to the treats afterward. We'd run together really fast.

Everyone said I had long legs for my body which gave me the ability to run really fast! He taught me lots of tricks. The one that most people talked about was when I'd jump into your hands. I enjoyed hugs and always wanted to be in the arms of any of my family members. Oooh, how I loved hugs. Hugs and heartbeats! Heartbeats and hugs!

One thing I really didn't like was being left alone. A few years after I came, we moved to a new bigger house. I was left alone a lot there as the family seemed to fall apart. My first daddy and big brother ended up leaving my mother and me all alone in that big house. When my mother would go out to work, I'd be all alone for a very long time.

I really didn't like that although I'd spend a lot of time lying in her bed waiting.

One day, a very nice guy who'd been to the house before took me to a big house in another city about an hour or so away. I stayed with him and two others, a young boy and girl. My mother ended up coming up with me and staying also. We were one big happy family. It was just another family!

It got even better because I was left for a while by myself except not as long. Since it was not just my mother and me, I'd wait for the boy and girl to come home. They always came first, then my new daddy and my mommy. These were good times! Especially when my new daddy's daddy came. I thought he was visiting, but he ended up staying. Now I really wasn't left alone long. I was so happy!

For several years, it was Grandfather (as the young boy and girl called him) and me left to take care of the house while the rest of the family went to work and school. He'd let me out and walk around the house with me until I took what he'd report as a "big dump". Sometimes he'd even point out where it was. The funny thing is he never picked it up! It was great as he'd let me run in the neighbor's yard and do what I had to do. We went out often. I always looked forward to it! I loved the grass and sunshine!

One day, Grandfather seemed to forget which way to go. He'd gotten lost with me once but luckily had this thing called a cell phone. Somebody called to see where he was and came and got us. Whew!

It wasn't long after that he had to leave. They said it was dangerous for him to stay in the house alone as he'd gotten lost a lot and further away each time. It was said when he had to go to the hospital, it was something called Alzheimer's disease. That's when you forget a lot…a whole lot, like where you are, who you are, where your house is located. Grandfather sometimes forgot who he was, where he was and where our home was.

Several years went by that he was gone. I ended up having other people come in and take great care of me; they would walk and feed me while my new daddy and my mommy were away on trips.

What was cool was my first big brother DeVaughn came to stay with us for a few years. I got to spend time with him and he walked me and ran with me like we used to do. He was the best trainer and friend.

As the years progressed, we had such great times! I remember when I'd jump in the car and ride with my mother to different places. She always had a big truck so I'd sit in her lap and watch as she drove.

DR. MONICA YOUNG ANDREWS

When I got tired, I'd lie down in her lap and get some rest. A lot of times she'd get to our destination and then I knew to jump in the back seat while she did what she needed to do. They always said I was a good dog. Funny thing I'd heard my mother say, "I never even wanted a dog, but I was so good that she kept me from her first marriage". Sometimes she'd even say that I minded better than my first daddy and big brother. People would just laugh!

I loved my family and I felt they loved me. As I grew older, things got a little different. My mother never really took me for walks. Then all of a sudden, we'd go for walks almost every day. I believe she was trying to stay healthy or something like that.

I just loved walking! We walked very long times especially when it was cool outside. My mommy used to walk me late at night as well when it was just she and I. And we both loved walking fast. She was really good at picking up my poop. No matter where we were, I always had to wait for her to fill her poop bag. Sometimes I'd go three times on a walk! That sure felt good!

Somewhere near my 12th birthday, I started staying with my Auntie Lorraine and Auntie Kathy. They were super cool!

I was on this really strict diet. From early on Auntie Lorraine would give me rice if I didn't eat what she put down for me. I really loved going to stay with them when my family left. I believe they loved me just as much! Although I had my own bed; they'd let me sleep in their bed just like my mommy and daddy! Thank God for my new daddy! My old daddy wasn't having me in the bed ever.

HEARTBEATS & HUGS

One day I started having a very bad cough. They said it sounded like somebody with emphysema which I learned was a type of lung condition. It was mostly a result of smoking cigarettes which of course I had never smoked anything, but wondered why I was feeling so bad.

It was close to the end of October because my mommy had a business trip and was leaving the day after Halloween. She took me to the vet for an emergency appointment where they x-rayed my chest and found something not too good.

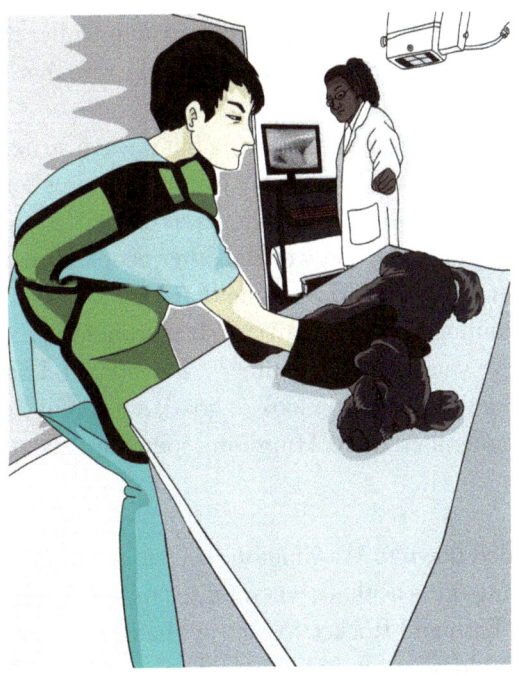

They recommended that she take me to a specialist. When she got back and took me to the specialist, it ended up being something called carcinoma cancer. They said it grew very fast. I could feel something happening, but I still wanted to play and walk. It was strange because as much as I wanted to, I couldn't even meet any family member at the door anymore. I mean I was right there before they'd open the door for years, but now it wasn't so easy for me. I didn't know what to think and neither did they.

My mommy took me to a holistic doggy doctor over an hour away where they did an ultraviolet (UV) ozone treatment. She ordered all these holistic supplements and food to work on killing the cancer. One thing she didn't realize was my lungs were filling up with fluid and neither the treatment nor the supplements could help with that.

We made it through Thanksgiving but it was a struggle. I even got to see Grandfather. He was in a nursing home and didn't look too well, though. I was carried in a tote bag so I would not disturb any of the other people. I remember getting in the room and realizing that I knew this guy. I started sniffing and realized Wow! It's Grandfather! "Where've you been all this time?", I wondered. Looking closer, I noticed he didn't look so good, not sure if he even saw or remembered me. Hmmmm, something seemed strange!

We headed down to Washington, D.C. to see more family. I liked going there as that's when I'd see my two doggie cousins, Basil and Rocket. We always had fun together and I was the oldest of all. I was the only one who could jump in my mommy's arms. I liked looking down at them from her arms.

HEARTBEATS & HUGS

Well, I had lots of coughing episodes in D.C. on Thanksgiving day. That is when my wheezing started with many of my breaths. My mommy took me to the emergency doggy hospital the next day and they gave me something called oxygen. The oxygen helped me breath much better. She had them do a procedure to drain the fluid out of my lungs. As I've said before she really, really loved me.

I think those doctors and nurses suggested something called euthanasia, whatever that is. That was the second time I'd heard that word as it sounded complicated, but my mommy opted to have the chest tap which I found out later cost her a lot of money. I ended up staying overnight so they could see if the fluid started accumulating again and at what rate. They said normally it accumulates in a couple of weeks.

Well, the fluid accumulated much quicker and I overheard my mommy praying to God about not wanting to make decisions that He should be making. "Decisions of life and death are YOUR decisions not ours", she shouted. She asked God for help. I believe I heard her pray and then say perhaps when Grandfather passes, then she would make that hard decision to euthanize (again, whatever that means).

On the morning of the following Tuesday, November 28, 2017, my mommy read a text message that Grandfather had passed during the night and again she went into prayer. She made a phone call to Banfield and at about 12 noon, I learned the meaning of euthanize. It was to make the decision to put me to sleep forever where I had no more pain, but would never see, touch or feel my family again. Banfield was really good with us. They said my mommy could stay with me as long as she wanted. I remember her smell as I fell off to sleep forever.

HEARTBEATS & HUGS

Although I was kind of glad not to be in any more pain, it really hurt to sense the pain of my mommy having to make that hard decision and to think about not feeling any more heartbeats or hugs from her.

I hope that my family will always remember my heartbeat and my hugs.

I further hope that reading my story comforts anyone who has ever had to or who may have to make the hard decision to euthanize their beloved family member.

Love with Heartbeat & Hugs,

Apollo ❣️

IN MEMORY OF

**Grandfather born Feb. 25, 1948
Apollo born Apr. 8, 2005**

Transitioned Nov. 28, 2017

ABOUT THE AUTHOR

Chaplain Dr. Monica Young Andrews the oldest of three, grew up in the District of Columbia, America's national capital. She attended private school and is a proud Hampton University alumnus. Although her background is in computer science, she's been in the financial arena for over ten years and has always been a practicing advocate of the application of knowledge. At age fifteen after receiving her first paycheck, she quickly learned about "Uncle Sam", but didn't understand why he was taking so much of her money, since she didn't even have an uncle named Sam!

Since 2010, she has worked fervently to equip thousands with the knowledge, tools and resources necessary to create everlasting wealth for true legacy building. She realized long ago that if she can ask ten people a question to which at least 80 percent know the answer, then why does she need to retain that information? Instead, she needs to know what those ten people do not. She has thus spent decades learning and practicing what the average person doesn't know. This may come in the form of credit repair and restoration, asset protection, tax benefits, the infinite banking concept, personal and business credit worthiness, day-to-day best practices, business funding, franchising, and book writing.

Because of her recognized contributions over the last

twenty-plus years, she was respectfully nominated to receive her honorary doctorate from Global Oved Dei Seminary (GODSU) in 2016. Those contributions include her other books, *RESPECT: What Does It Mean To You?*, a book for teenagers, parents or anyone who has ever felt disrespected, and *All in Divine Order: Nothing Happens by Accident*, where she shares life experiences that grew her faith beyond measure moving her into purpose in hopes of guiding readers into their purpose using their life experiences.

Additional contributions include Divine Order, which supports the Divine Order Network and Spirnancial Partners in Shine movements, as well as the Divine Order Foundation. She has put these together to elevate the Spirnancial well-being of humanity, one person, family, community and company at a time, through education, tools and experience. Dr. Andrews is a true example of a "real teacher" defined in the book *Fake* by Robert Kiyosaki, author of *Rich Dad, Poor Dad*. Chaplain Dr. Monica Andrews enjoys spending time with her family, traveling and making a difference wherever God leads her. Prayerfully, you'll join the Divine Order movement!

"Knowledge is power; however,
the APPLICATION of Knowledge
makes You POWERFUL".
-Chaplain Dr. Monica Young Andrews

Continue to move full of POWER

▶ youtube.com/divineordernetwork
a amazon.com/author/divineorder

www.ingramcontent.com/pod-product-compliance
Lightning Source LLC
Chambersburg PA
CBHW052017160426
42811CB00116B/522